To Anna

Copyright © 1982 by Douglas Florian

Library of Congress Cataloging in Publication Data

Florian, Douglas.
  The City.

  Summary: A woman carrying a shopping bag passes all
the sights of the city on the way to her apartment.
[1. Stories without words.   2. City and town life —
Pictorial works]   I. Title.
PZ7.F6645Ci 1982   [E]   81-43312
ISBN 0-690-04166-7   AACR2
ISBN 0-690-04167-5 (lib. bdg.)

1 2 3 4 5 6 7 8 9 10
First Edition

THE CITY

DOUGLAS FLORIAN

Thomas Y. Crowell   **New York**